SELAH MOMENTS

McDougal & Associates
Servants of Christ and Stewards of the Mysteries of God

SELAH MOMENTS

by

MARILYN MCDANIEL

Selah Moments
Copyright © 2018—Marilyn McDaniel
ALL RIGHTS RESERVED

Unless otherwise noted, all Scripture references are from *The Amplified Bible, Classic Edition,* copyright © 1954, 1958, 1962, 1964, 1965, 1987 by The Lockman Foundation, La Habra, California. References marked "NKJV" are from *The Holy Bible, New King James Version*, copyright © 1979, 1980, 1982, by Thomas Nelson, Inc., Nashville, Tennessee. References marked "KJV" are from the *Holy Bible, King James Version,* public domain.

McDougal & Associates is an organization dedicated to spreading the Gospel of the Lord Jesus Christ to as many people as possible in the shortest time possible.

Published by:

McDougal & Associates
188965 Greenwell Springs Road
Greenwell Springs, LA 70739

www.thepublishedword.com

ISBN: 978-1-940461-97-7

Printed in the U.S., the U.K. and Australia
For Worldwide Distribution

> *A word fitly spoken ... is like apples of gold in settings of silver.*
> Proverbs 25:11

DEDICATION

I would like to dedicate this book to my children—Chassity, Joshua, Tonya and Jonathon—who are my precious blessings from the Lord. I am thankful for each of them, as well as my grandchildren. My prayer is that this book be a blessing to them, as well as to all who read it.

CONTENTS

Introduction 9

1. A Prepared People 11
2. The Captain of Our Salvation 13
3. Draw Near to God 16
4. Have You Been "Kissed"? 18
5. Justice Is Your Portion 21
6. The Lord, Our Maker 24
7. Personally Yours 26
8. What Condition Is Your Condition In? 28
9. Whine or Dine? 33
10. The Barren Shall Produce 35
11. The Desperate Pursuit 37
12. Times N Seasons 41
13. Tombstone or Stepping Stone? 42
14. Turn It Around 44
15. Zealous Fear 47
16. Work's Reward 49

17. Resurrection Power 51
18. Return and Turn 52
19. Praise Him in the Process 55
20. Purr-fected or Perfected? 57
21. The Right Season, Time, Place and People 59
22. Soul Conversion 61
23. Step Up, Step Out and Step Over 63
24. The Lord Awoke 65
25. Worship Bridges the Gap 67
26. Onesiphorus 69
27. Bars of Brass Are Broken 71
28. A Breaker's Anointing 73
29. Don't Mess with My Kids 74
30. Embrace Your Day 76
31. Fret or Faith? 81
32. Fine-Tune Discernment 83

Author Contact Page 86

INTRODUCTION

Selah, a word used in the Bible in the book of Psalms, is translated in the Classic Version of the Amplified Bible as *"Pause and think about it."* My hope is that you will take the *Selah Moments* written within this book and pause and think on their message. May you find, in these pages, encouragement, revelation and comfort for your own journey with the Lord.

Before you read the words of this book, allow me to speak over you this Aaronic blessing, first given to the Israelite people thousands of years ago.

Numbers 6:25-26
> *The LORD make His face to shine upon and enlighten you and be gracious (kind, merciful, and giving favor) to you; the LORD lift up His [approving] countenance upon you and give you peace (tranquility of heart and life continually).*

Marilyn McDaniel

1

A PREPARED PEOPLE

Mark 13:27
> *And then He will send out the angels and will gather His elect (those He has picked out for Himself), from the four winds, from the farthest bounds of the earth to the farthest bounds of heaven.*

Beloved, Jesus is coming at a time we least expect it. He will gather His people, His chosen ones, to Himself, those who heard the call and made the choice to be His people and to let Him be their God, just like the children of Israel, as they were called out of Egypt to a land of God's promise, where they would be His people, and He would be their God.

We, too, have been called out of this world, from the darkness of the world system and from a worldly lifestyle, to become God's chosen ones in His Kingdom. But consider the ten virgins. Only five of them were prepared, having their lamps trimmed and filled with fresh oil, making sure they continued to burn with expectancy. When the groom came, they went in with him, and the door was shut!

Selah Moments

Who are the "elect"? The elect are those who are committed daily to the will, plan, pursuit and purpose of God in their daily living while here on earth. They are those who live in anticipation of His coming, conducting their lives in a manner befitting Kingdom living in holiness and righteous. They are those who conduct their lives on a high moral plane, not giving in to the seductions of the flesh.

Paul wrote:

Galatians 5:24
> *And those who belong to Christ Jesus (the Messiah) have crucified the flesh (that godless human nature) with its passions, appetite and desires.*

Some of these passions, appetites and desires are listed in the previous verses:

Galatians 5:19-21
> *Now the doings (practicing) of the flesh are clear (obvious): they are immorality, impurity and indecency, idolatry, sorcery, enmity, strife, jealousy, anger (ill temper), selfishness, divisions (dissensions), party spirit (factions, sects with peculiar opinions, heresies), envy, drunkenness, carousing, and the like.*

A Prepared People

Those who are prepared for Christ's coming conduct their lives in such a way to show forth Holy Spirit fruit:

Galatians 5:22-23
> *But the fruit of the [Holy] Spirit [the work which His presence within accomplishes] is love, joy (gladness), peace, patience (an even temper, forbearance), kindness, goodness (benevolence), faithfulness, gentleness (meekness, humility), self-control (self-restraint, continence).*

Beloved, if we are called out from a life of darkness and called into a life of righteousness, holiness and godliness, how then should we conduct ourselves in preparedness for Christ's coming?

Let us take note: daily we need to take up our cross (crucifying the fleshly and its unholy, ungodly desires and passions) and pursuing the Holy Spirit in us for guidance, strength, grace, mercy, truth and godly living that is pleasing to our heavenly Father, in righteousness, peace and joy in the Holy Ghost!

SELAH!

∽ 2 ∝

THE CAPTAIN OF OUR SALVATION

Hebrews 2:10
> *For it was an act worthy [of God] and fitting [to the divine nature] that He, for Whose sake and by Whom all things have their existence, in bringing many sons into glory, should make the Pioneer of their salvation perfect [should bring to maturity the human experience necessary to be perfectly equipped for His office as High Priest] through suffering.*

Jesus has been made the Captain of our salvation through His sufferings. He was known as *"a man of sorrows."* He endured the cross, despising the shame, for the joy set before Him:

Hebrews 12:2
> *He, for the joy [of obtaining the prize] that was set before Him, endured the cross, despising and ignoring the shame, and is now seated at the right hand of the throne of God.*

The Captain Of Our Salvation

That joy, was you and I.

Jesus was not excited about the beatings He had to bear (the tearing of His flesh), nor about being crucified on the cross. The weightiness of His body pulled Him down onto the nails in His hands and feet and made it difficult for Him to breathe. None of this was joyful. Still, He endured all of this for the joy set before Him.

What was that promised joy?

1. His Father made Him a promise that He would not leave His soul in Hell, but that He would be resurrected.
2. That His resurrection would pave the way for others to be born into the Kingdom of God.

Jesus' suffering birthed sons and daughters. That includes you and me. We are His joy!

SELAH!

ೞ 3 ೞ

DRAW NEAR TO GOD

Psalm 73:28

*But it is good for me to draw near to God; I have put my trust in the L*ORD *God and made Him my refuge, that I may declare all Your works.*

For the Lord would say:

Come, draw near to Me with your whole heart. Let Me bear you up in My strong arm in the day of your adversity. See if I will not prove Myself to you. I am He who upholds you. Yes, I am He who upholds you in the day of provocation that has come to test and try your hearts. Yes, see that My desire is upon you, to save you, to deliver you, to strengthen you, that you be not overcome, but rather that you overcome.

You must draw near to Me, and I will draw near to you. Trust Me to deliver you and make a way of escape for you!

Draw Near To God

Declare My goodness among the hearers. Watch and see My provision on your behalf. For surely I will deliver you. Surely I will draw near to you, as you draw near to Me! Only declare My works! For they will speak, and I will perform!

Saith your Father!

SELAH!

৯ 4 ෬

HAVE YOU BEEN "KISSED"?

Psalm 85:10

Mercy and loving-kindness and truth have met together; righteousness and peace have kissed each other.

The Scriptures teach that we are trees of righteousness and are destined to flourish in the earth. We have been made righteous by the unveiling of the truth of Christ Jesus. It was because of God's mercy that truth was brought into the earth, for all men everywhere to embrace and come into right standing with Father God, Creator of Heaven and earth.

James 2:13

For to him who has shown no mercy the judgment [will be] merciless, but mercy [full of glad confidence] exults victoriously over judgment.

Have You Been "Kissed"?

Mercy triumphs over judgement! From Adam to Jesus, humanity was judged and condemned to a sentence of death, Hell and the grave. But God extended a hand of mercy because of His great love:

John 3:16
> *For God so greatly loved and dearly prized the world that He [even] gave up His only begotten ([a]unique) Son, so that whoever believes in (trusts in, clings to, relies on) Him shall not perish (come to destruction, be lost) but have eternal (everlasting) life.*

This made the way for *"whosoever will"* to be reconciled to, brought back into right standing with God, and that was His intent from the foundation of the world.

Mercy and truth met through the sacrifice of Christ. Righteousness and peace kissed by His resurrection. Thus, the kiss of life everlasting was released, for all humanity to be right with Father God and to be at peace for all eternity.

God is saying:

> *Some of you need to be kissed again!*
> *You need to meet with mercy and truth.*
> *Be kissed with righteousness and peace!*

Selah Moments

Wherever you are today and whatever you are experiencing, Father wants to kiss you with His love, mercy, truth and grace!

SELAH!

♊ 5 ♋

JUSTICE IS YOUR PORTION!

Psalm 37:1

Fret not ... .

To *fret* is "to become agitated, disturbed, eaten up with or troubled by." What is it that we are not to allow to disturb us? It is the *"evildoers"* who are seemingly getting away with their evil deeds and the immeasurable injustice of it all. Do not let this consume you, for fretting will cause you harm!

Verse 8 repeats this admonition:

Psalm 37:8

Fret not yourself—it tends only to evildoing.

Why? Because it brews bitterness and vexation of the soul! It clouds the mind. It cripples the heart, bringing bitter poison to your body.

Understand that God is a just God and that, in the end, justice will prevail. He Himself will deal with this evil and the works of evildoers.

Selah Moments

As for us, we are to trust Him with all of our heart and mind:

Psalm 37:3
Trust (lean on, rely on, and be confident) in the Lord and do good; so shall you dwell in the land and feed surely on His faithfulness, and truly you shall be fed.

Trust in God in reliance upon His faithfulness and truth. He is our Vindicator, our Provider, our Protector, our Deliverer and the One who maintains our cause and brings us justice.

"Do good," that which is right and righteous.

We are to delight ourselves in the Lord:

Psalm 37:4
Delight yourself also in the Lord, and He will give you the desires and secret petitions of your heart.

We are to commit everything to Him:

Psalm 37:5
Commit your way to the Lord [roll and repose each care of your load on Him]; trust (lean on, rely on, and be confident) also in Him and He will bring it to pass.

Justice Is Your Portion!

We are to rest in Him:

Psalm 37:7
> *Be still and rest in the Lord; wait for Him and patiently lean yourself upon Him; fret not yourself because of him who prospers in his way, because of the man who brings wicked devices to pass.*

Our confidence in God is to be with a laid-back peace and assurance that He's got this! This will work to our favor and just cause! So whatever the evil doers are doing and whatever the naysayers are saying, trust, delight and rest in the Lord, for justice is our portion!

SELAH!

೩ 6 ೨

THE LORD, OUR MAKER

Psalm 95:6
> *O come, let us worship and bow down, let us kneel before the Lord our Maker [in reverent praise and supplication].*

Our Father, in His infinite wisdom and desire, created us. He formed us in our mother's womb. He fashioned us with intricate detail, from the color of our skin, the color of our eyes, the color of our hair and the shape of our bodies. We were intricately designed by Him, and we are the seed of His reflection.

We were formed, created, in God's image and likeness. When you look in the mirror, know that you are a reflection of your Daddy, God! Know that He delights or takes pleasure in you. Know that His desire, plan and purpose is for your wellbeing, that His thoughts are for good and not evil, that He has a future and hope for all your comings and goings, and that in Him you are being groomed for His purpose and your own wellbeing.

You are not a mere happenstance! You were purposed *by* God Almighty and *for* God Almighty. Your very existence

The Lord, Our Maker

was preordained by Him. He purposed you, and your life on the earth is for His presence, for His dwelling—He in you and you in Him.

Father God gave of Himself for you, so now you need to give Him of yourself. Allow Him to manage your life. Allow Him to lead you and direct you. Allow Him to fully posses you for His glory. He is your Daddy, and He will not withhold any good thing from you.

Let us bow the knee of our hearts in honor and respect to Him, for He alone is a faithful Creator and the Bishop and Shepherd of our souls.

Paul wrote:

Ephesians 3:14-15

For this reason [seeing the greatness of this plan by which you are built together in Christ], I bow my knees before the Father of our Lord Jesus Christ, for Whom every family in heaven and on earth is named [that Father from Whom all fatherhood takes its title and derives its name].

Life is a mystery, but only to those outside the truth and the reality of God. To those of us who are on the inside, He reveals Himself and brings enlightenment, showing us the way of life. For He is Life, our God, our Maker!

SELAH!

ೞ 7 ಛ

PERSONALLY YOURS

John 3:16
For God so greatly loved and dearly prized the world {YOU} that He [even] gave up His only begotten (unique) Son, so that whoever believes in (trusts in, clings to, relies on) Him shall not perish (come to destruction, be lost) but have eternal (everlasting) life.

Beloved, none of us is happenstance! We are all God's creation. The day you were placed in your mother's womb, God the Father, God the Son and God the Holy Spirit made a personal decree with each other for a redemptive work for your eternal existence!

You have been personally and intricately fashioned and ordained by the Father for a plan, a purpose and a destiny. And not for evil, but for eternal good. In that plan, Jesus, the Son, came to earth and personally took for you the result of your sin. He took your sickness and disease in His body. He accepted your penalty of death, Hell and the grave, and He did it personally for you!

The Holy Spirit personally took up residence in you, and He has personally empowered you to live out your preor-

Personally Yours

dained and God-given destiny in the earth. How personable is that?

Now, let me ask you a question: How personally have you taken God's love, His mercy, His grace extended to you? How personally grateful are you for Jesus' sacrifice that you might live and not die eternally apart from God? How personally are you fellowshipping with the Holy Spirit in you to lead, guide and direct your way in the earth for the provisions and blessings God has poured out on you?

Beloved, let us make a personal note, take the time and make the effort to personally seek God. Seek His presence. Seek His destiny for your life. Seek His will and His plan. Answer His pursuit of you!

Personally seek the Kingdom of God and the fellowship of the Spirit, in humility and with a grateful attitude for the personal interest God has taken *in* you and *for* you. Give thanks for the personal sacrifice of Jesus Christ for you!

SELAH!

8

WHAT CONDITION IS YOUR CONDITION IN?

1 Corinthians 11:31-32
> *For if we searchingly examined ourselves [detecting our shortcomings and recognizing our own condition], we should not be judged and penalty decreed [by the divine judgment]. But when we [fall short and] are judged by the Lord, we are disciplined and chastened, so that we may not [finally] be condemned [to eternal punishment along] with the world.*

We are living in the dispensation of God's grace, but there is coming an appointed time when grace will be lifted, and the judgement of God will prevail. This judgement will begin with the household of God, those of us who profess to be Christians (see 1 Peter 4:17).

In Revelation 2 and 3, Jesus was judging the condition of the seven churches of Asia. These churches are a representation of the condition of His Church today, and He is giving ample warning to those who are not in a rightful condition

What Condition Is Your Condition In?

with Him, who is the Head of the Church, to repent and get right while there is time.

1. Ephesus was the church that had lost her first love. She had some good works, she hated evil, and she tested false prophets. But when it came to her personal intimacy with God, her relationship with Him, and when it came to her fire and zeal for God, it became apparent that she had become cold and indifferent. Her lamp was going out, and her effectiveness in the earth had grown dim.

2. Pergamos was the compromising church. She dwelt where Satan's throne was. Her members held the Lord's name and declared faith in Him, but they also held the doctrine of Balaam and were guilty of practicing idolatry and committing sexual immorality.
They also held to the doctrines of the Nicolaitans, doctrines of occult paganism. They taught that a person could practice the deeds of a sinful nature while still embracing Christianity. That reminds us of the perverted teachings on grace that we hear today, that a person can sin all he wants, and grace has him covered. What a foul perverted doctrine!

3 Thyatira was the corrupt church. Her members did many works of love, service, faith and patience, but they did

Selah Moments

not deal with the sin issues. They allowed a Jezebel spirit to remain in their leadership in the practice of sexual immorality and idolatry.

4. Sardis was the dead church. She had a name that she was alive, but God said she was dead. In other words, her members professed to be Christians, but they bore no fruit of actually being followers of Christ.

5. Laodicea was the lukewarm Church. Her members were rich with this world's goods, and they lived a good moral life. But they leaned more on this than on their need for God. Consequently, Jesus had something against them and He called them to repentance before the final Judgement, giving them fair warning to deal with these issues right then, before He would come.

The final two churches, our Lord commended and encouraged:

6. Smyrna was the persecuted church. God saw that the believers in Smyrna had come through much tribulation, many trials and much poverty. Satan had tried to destroy them, but they had not bent nor bowed under his pressure, Instead, they had endured patiently. Therefore, the Lord assured them, a crown of life awaited them!

What Condition Is Your Condition In?

7. Philadelphia was the faithful church. The believers there had persevered in God's commandments, had not denied His name and had kept His Word. Therefore, He promised them, *"I also will keep you [safe] from the hour of trial (testing) which is coming on the whole world to try those who dwell upon the earth"* (Revelation 3:10).

Paul wrote to the Corinthian believers:

2 Corinthians 3:5
For if we searchingly examined ourselves [detecting our shortcomings and recognizing our own condition], we should not be judged and penalty decreed [by the divine judgment].

Where are you? What condition would you find yourself in if Christ were to come today. As we can see, ninety percent of the professing Church is not ready. Heed the wisdom of Solomon:

Proverbs 9:6
Leave off, simple ones [forsake the foolish and simple-minded] and live! And walk in the way of insight and understanding.

Selah Moments

Jesus said to all of the churches of Revelation 2 and 3 and, thus, for us all:

Revelation 3:11
I am coming quickly; hold fast what you have, so that no one may rob you and deprive you of your crown.

SELAH!

∞ 9 ∞

WHINE OR DINE?

Proverbs 26:13
The sluggard says, There is a lion in the way! A lion is in the streets!

When someone says, "There is a lion in the street," the simple pass on, giving no heed.

When Jesus ascended back to Heaven, He released the empowerment of the Holy Spirit *in* us and *upon* us, to be more than conquerors in the earth. As always, the enemy goes about like a lion, seeking whom he may devour. But Jesus stripped him of power and authority against us. Still, many times, when the enemy comes near us, we fall down, whine and lick our wounds.

According to Psalm 23, the Lord has prepared a table for us in the very presence of our enemies. That table has all the necessary nutrients for our nourishment and sustenance against the evil one. It is filled with the Word of God, which brings healing, breakthrough, strength, courage, endurance, strategy, peace, comfort, insight, mercy and grace!

Selah Moments

When we whine in our circumstances, we are devoured of the lion. But when we dine, we sit at the banquet table of the Lord and eat His Word, and it carries us our current circumstances and carries us over to victory.

There is he who roars like a lion, and then there is He Who ROARS. Jesus has the real roar, and we are His lions in the earth. So dine and don't whine! Eat and roar the pleasantness of the Word eaten!

WOW! This perfect love that cast out fear sure is delicious! Yummm! I am healed by the stripes of Jesus! Ummmmhmmm! No weapon formed against me shall prosper! And that is only the beginning.

SELAH!

∽ 10 ∾

THE BARREN SHALL PRODUCE

Isaiah 54:1-3

> *Sing, O barren one, you who did not bear; break forth into singing and cry aloud, you who did not travail with child! For the [spiritual] children of the desolate one will be more than the children of the married wife, says the Lord. Enlarge the place of your tent, and let the curtains of your habitations be stretched out; spare not; lengthen your cords and strengthen your stakes, for you will spread abroad to the right hand and to the left; and your offspring will possess the nations and make the desolate cities to be inhabited.*

If you have been experiencing barrenness in your endeavors, and you feel like you are on the backside of the desert and nothing is happening, GET READY! You are about to produce from your barrenness. You are about to experience fruitfulness that you did not know existed for you.

Selah Moments

God told the barren woman to sing loudly. Why? Because she was about to bear children of the Spirit kind. Her fruitfulness would go beyond the natural and into the supernatural.

Therefore, she was told to enlarge her tent, the place of her dwelling, and to make room for more. Why? Because God was about to bring fruitfulness to her barrenness, and she would need more room to contain the coming fruit.

The enlarging of our tents signifies making more room in our hearts for more of God's presence, more worship, more praise, more attitude of thanksgiving, more Holy Spirit yielding and fellowship, and this will all result in our flourishing, moving from barrenness to fruitfulness!

And I say to you:

> Get ready!
> This barren place is about to bring forth fruit!

SELAH!

ॐ 11 ॐ

THE DESPERATE PURSUIT

Luke 5:19
> *But finding no way to bring him in because of the crowd, they went up on the roof and lowered him with his stretcher through the tiles into the midst in front of Jesus.*

When a person is desperate, it is because they have the sense or feeling that something has to give or destruction will surely come. To be desperate is to desire that which seems unattainable. We sing a song: "Lord, I am desperate for You!" This relates to a heart condition, a holy, hot desire, a passion for God's holy presence in your life.

A desperate believer is so desperate to have God's glory manifested *in* them and *through* them that whatever measure it takes on their part, they are willing to do it. Even when it is hard, difficult and uncomfortable, they are ready.

Luke 5 is a true story of desperation and desire in which four men traveled to where Jesus was, carrying their paralytic friend on a stretcher between them, so that he could be healed. The problem was that when they got to the place

Selah Moments

where Jesus was teaching, they could not get to Him because of the crowd around Him.

But these men were desperate, so they took desperate measures, climbing up on the roof of the house where Jesus was teaching, tearing up the roof and letting their friend down through the hole they had created just in front of Jesus. They were just that determined for the touch of Jesus to heal their friend.

Despite the difficulties and the discomfort involved, they laid aside every excuse and sought a means by which they could accomplish their goal. Whatever it took they were ready to do it.

Let me ask you a question: How desperate are you for the presence of God in *your* life? How desperate are you for a move of God in *your* situation? If you are not desperate enough, you will not persist when things seem impossible. But, as the Scriptures assure us, *"All things are possible with God"* (Matthew 19:26) and *"All things can be (are possible) to him who believes"* (Mark 9:23).

These four men believed in Jesus' ability to heal their friend. They were desperate, and they would not take no for an answer. Thus, they pursued their goal till they found a way to see it accomplished.

What these men did was not comfortable or easy, but their desperation to have Jesus heal their friend caused them to pursue Him despite every difficulty. And the result was that

The Desperate Pursuit

their friend was healed.

You and I also need to become desperate for the promises of God to us, those promises that He said were *"yes"* and *"amen"* (2 Corinthians 1:20, NKJV). We must be desperate enough that we will endure whatever comes our way and pursue God's promises even when it is difficult and uncomfortable.

Joyce Meyer has said, "Live by the excuses; die by the reason!" Saints of God, sometimes it is uncomfortable and difficult as we pursue God's promises, as it was for these men carrying their friend. The crowd hindered them, so, in desperation, they had to find a way around the hindrance.

Many times, as we pursue God's promised provision of health, wealth, prosperity, well-being and eternal life while we are still here on earth, roadblocks or hindrances seem to stand in our way. When it happens, it is decision time. We must ask ourselves, "Am I going to give up and quit because something seems impossible, because there seems to be no breakthrough?" No, beloved, this is a time for desperate action on your part. We sometimes call them "desperate measures." This is a time to outsmart the hindrance and find a means to get around the roadblock, regardless of how uncomfortable it may be or how difficult it may seem.

You may find that the hinderance or roadblock to your desired blessing may be something in your lives that is standing in you way and needs to be abandoned. In this way, you

Selah Moments

can rid yourself of the difficulty and discomfort and clear your path to the promise.

How desperate are you?

SELAH!

~ 12 ~

TIMES N SEASONS

Ecclesiastes 3:1
To everything there is a season, and a time for every matter or purpose under heaven.

Proverbs 31:15 states that our times are in God's hand. Galatians 6:9 states that we will reap *"in DUE SEASON if we faint not."* Our part is to trust God for our time and season. How can we do that?

- Pay attention prayerfully, being sensitive to the Lord's leading.
- Move when He says to move!
- Give when He says to give!
- Release what He says to release!
- Stand still when He says to stand still!
- Be quiet when He says to be quiet!

Why? Because our times and seasons are in His hands! Therefore, trust Him in the process!

SELAH!

∽ 13 ∾

TOMBSTONE OR STEPPING STONE?

John 16:33
> *I have told you these things, so that in Me you may have [perfect] peace and confidence. In the world you have tribulation and trials and distress and frustration; but be of good cheer [take courage; be confident, certain, undaunted]! For I have overcome the world. [I have deprived it of power to harm you and have conquered it for you.]*

Many of us can say that we've had plenty of opportunities to overcome. Such times can either be a tombstone or a stepping stone in our lives. Jesus was saying that in Him we can have peace in the midst of any and every storm of life.

Whatever you may be facing that is bringing turmoil into your life right now, cling to Jesus. Allow Him to place stepping stones in your path. These stones will bring you to a place of victory.

What you are facing is sent by the enemy to be a

Tombstone or Stepping Stone?

tombstone, a destructive force, but through Christ you can overcome, doing valiantly. Make that tombstone into a stepping stone, and claim your victory in Christ Jesus!

SELAH!

∞ 14 ∞

TURN IT AROUND

Luke 4:8
> *And Jesus replied to him, Get behind Me, Satan! It is written, You shall do homage to and worship the Lord your God, and Him only shall you serve.*

In this way, Jesus turned the enemy's temptations around by speaking the Word of God against the tempter, and we can do the same today.

All of us are struggling with areas where the enemy is trying to thwart us, to move us off course. He speaks things to us that, in the natural realm, seem to be true.

Think of Elijah. He said, "God take me. Jezebel is after me, and I am the only one of Your prophets left. Now she wants to kill me" (see 1 Kings 19). The truth was that there were still one hundred prophets that Obadiah had taken and hidden in a cave, away from Jezebel's wrath (see 1 Kings 18).

All that Elijah knew in the natural was that Jezebel had slaughtered all of the prophets of God and was now

Turn It Around

after him. That's why he was begging God to take his life. He was thinking, "Lord, I am done! My life is over. Take me now." But God brought an angel to provided nourishment and strength for Elijah and, with them, He sent His Word, and the prophet survived.

Whatever the enemy is saying to you, whatever he is trying to convince you of, TURN IT AROUND. Speak the opposite of what he is saying.

- The enemy is saying that you are financially broke, but God says that He supplies all of your needs, and you have more than enough!
- The enemy is saying that God is not going to come through for your healing, but God says that healing is the children's bread! He wants you to declare, "By His stripes I am healed!"
- The enemy is saying that, like Elijah, you are all alone, but God says that there is a "great cloud of witnesses" around you, a company with which the Lord is now giving you a connection.
- The enemy is telling you that you are tired, but God says that the strength of Christ perfects you and the grace of God is sufficient for you!

These are all examples of how you can turn your situation around. Your voice will authenticate the reality of your situ-

Selah Moments

ation. Use it just like Jesus did against what seems to be true in natural realm, and speak the reality of the supernatural.

How can we do this? By putting on the warfare garment, girding our loins with the truth of God's Word!

Go ahead! Turn It Around!

SELAH!

≈ 15 ≈

ZEALOUS FEAR

Proverbs 23:17, NKJV
*Do not let your heart envy sinners,
But be zealous for the fear of the LORD all the day*

Zealous ... What does it mean? It means "excessive feelings or uncompromising enthusiasm." I like to call it the heat of desire or the passion of the heart. Jeremiah had a fire shut up in his bones. That's passion.

Zeal produces a fear, a reverential respect, adoration and admiration, and it is love and passion motivated. Our Lord Jesus was so passionate about us that He gave us a special recognition and attention. Our value to Him produced a zeal for our redemption and restored fellowship, and thus, He gave of Himself to us in His death, burial, resurrection and ascension.

Because our Father was so zealous for our relationship to be restored with Him, we, too, should be zealous in our respect and honor to Him. He is the One who seeded us, and we are His offspring.

Selah Moments

We can show our zeal for God by desiring to be close to Him, fellowship with Him, worship Him and desire to please Him, and we can do it all with excessive feelings and uncompromising enthusiasm, filled with the joy and glory of His will and divine pleasure!

SELAH

~ 16 ~

WORK'S REWARD

2 Chronicles 15:7
Be strong, therefore, and let not your hands be weak and slack, for your work shall be rewarded.

The Father would say to us, those who busy themselves with Kingdom business:

I am aware of all your doings:

- Each time you declare My goodness
- Each time you bow the knee of your heart to pray for something or someone
- Each time you reach your hand out to the poor
- Each time you lay hands on the sick
- Each time you finance My sent ones to go out into the harvest field

I am aware, and I am He who rewards:

- Those who obey Me and seek Me

Selah Moments

- Those who commit to walking uprightly
- Those who commit to expanding My Kingdom

I am He who sees and He who rewards thee. Therefore, remain strong and do not let your hands become weak. For there is a reward for all your works!

SELAH

⚡ 17 ⚡

RESURRECTION POWER

Romans 6:4
We were buried therefore with Him by the baptism into death, so that just as Christ was raised from the dead by the glorious [power] of the Father, so we too might [habitually] live and behave in newness of life.

As Christians, we are grafted into the family of God through the acceptance of Jesus Christ as our personal Lord and Savior. This is just as the nation of Israel experienced before leaving Egypt in the Exodus. The death angel passed over them, and they were released from the stronghold of Egyptian bondage, released to go forth and worship their God.

God then led them to the Promised Land, and on the way, He would reveal Himself as the One who covered them, the One who guided them, the One who gave them great victories over every enemy and the One who provided all of their personal needs.

Jesus, our Redeemer, took with Him the keys of death, Hell and the grave when He rose from the dead, and with

Selah Moments

that, He rendered all demonic forces powerless against the people of God. This power of the resurrection was the work of the third Person of the Trinity, the Holy Spirit Himself! This same Holy Spirit resurrection power was released to believers on the Day of Pentecost and is available to us today.

Jesus had said that when He would ascend, He would then send the Holy Spirit as power through a baptism of fire, and it came upon all those who waited in the Upper Room that day. Jesus demonstrated, in His resurrection, power over all sin, sickness, disease, death, Hell, the grave and all demonic forces, and this same power has been released to you and me. We are empowered by the Holy Spirit so that we can rise above all the dictates of our flesh and sin, and so that we can heal the sick, raise the dead and cast out demons.

This resurrected power is *in* us and works *through* us so that we may demonstrate that the Kingdom of God is at hand in the earth, by signs, wonders and miracles!

SELAH!

∞ 18 ∞

RETURN AND TURN

Isaiah 30:15
> *For thus said the Lord God, the Holy One of Israel: In returning [to Me] and resting [in Me] you shall be saved; in quietness and in [trusting] confidence shall be your strength. But you would not.*

God in saying:

> You have been like the woman who had the issue of blood and had spent all her money on doctors, but had found no cure. Finally, she reached out to touch the hem of Jesus' garment, and instantly she was healed.
> You have tried all the worldly counsel and wisdom, only to find no cure for your dilemma.

God is also saying:

Selah Moments

TURN AND RETURN to Me. Get quiet before Me! I will strengthen you. I will instruct you. I will guide you in the right way.

Isaiah 30:21
And your ears will hear a word behind you, saying, This is the way; walk in it, when you turn to the right hand and when you turn to the left.

There is an invitation here to turn to God. Get quite, and hear from Him. In His presence you will find the strength, the cure, and the direction you are in need of!

Selah!

≈ 19 ≈

PRAISE HIM IN THE PROCESS

Psalm 27:6
And now shall my head be lifted up above my enemies round about me; in His tent I will offer sacrifices and shouting of joy; I will sing, yes, I will sing praises to the Lord.

Many times the enemy attacks us with fear, doubt and unbelief concerning prayers through which we are believing God for something. These things that he uses bring hopelessness, depression and oppression.

It is time to fight against the enemy of your soul and to deny that human sense and reason that makes you look upon the natural circumstances. These are sent to avert the soul away from the promises of God, which are Yes and Amen to the believer.

Your warfare is to offer a sacrifice of praise. The reason it is a sacrifice is that nothing in you wants to praise God. Indeed, everything in you wants to quit, to give up. Your soul is bent toward the lie of the enemy.

Selah Moments

Bend your soul toward praise, and God's Spirit will raise you up. In praise, confidence, faith and trust will arise, and, as your soul prospers, so will you, in that for which you are believing!

SELAH!

20

PURR-FECTED OR PERFECTED?

Hebrews 6:1
> *Therefore let us go on and get past the elementary stage in the teachings and doctrine of Christ (the Messiah), advancing steadily toward the completeness and perfection that belong to spiritual maturity. Let us not again be laying the foundation of repentance and abandonment of dead works (dead formalism) and of the faith [by which you turned] to God.*

As I was out and about today, worshipping and praying, these two words came to me. As I began to meditate, I began to see what God was saying. He used the example of a cat when it is being rubbed. As the cat's body is being rubbed, the cat stretches and purrs. It is enjoying the appeasement of its body rub. When the rubbing stops, the cat will begin to purr and rub up against the person who was appeasing his body with the comfort of rubbing.

Selah Moments

God showed me that is what it is like when we go after the appeasement of our flesh. While our flesh is being appeased, we purr like kittens. But, once the appeasement is over, we begin to purr for that appeasement again. What we do not realize is that the one giving the pleasure of fleshly appeasement is an enemy called destruction and corruption.

Picture this: You are purring with the appeasement of the flesh, and you take a look and see that a demon is actually doing the stroking. While making you purr, it has an evil grin on it face, knowing that it has you just where it wants you. It has purr-fected you into its demonic influence and away from what Christ has made you free from.

Todd White states: "We are not called to be confessing Christians, but possessed by Christ, in a new and living lifestyle of holiness and righteousness."

In Hebrews 6, Paul was encouraging the Jewish believers to move on from repentance and dead works unto perfection. We are to mature and grow in Christ in a more perfect way, not being caught up in the deceitful lusts of fleshly appeasement, but growing and maturing in Christian living that brings forth the peaceable fruit of righteousness!

SELAH!

21

THE RIGHT SEASON, TIME, PLACE AND PEOPLE

Matthew 20:6
> *And about the eleventh hour (five o'clock) he went out and found still others standing around, and said to them, Why do you stand here idle all day?*

It was the eleventh hour of the day, and those who were standing by were called to work in the harvest field.
Jesus said:

John 4:35
> *Do you not say, It is still four months until harvest time comes? Look! I tell you, raise your eyes and observe the fields and see how they are already white for harvesting.*

The field is white unto harvest, we are the people called to do the harvesting, and this is the time for reaping. It is harvest time, wherever you happen to be and whatever you happen to be doing at the moment.

Selah Moments

This is the eleventh hour, and a harvest of souls is ripe and ready to be reaped. Be God's voice to them. Be God's touch to them. Be God's provision for them. Be God's power for healing and deliverance for them.

Be the person God can use. Be at the right place, and be with the right connections. It's harvest time!

SELAH!

ക 22 ര

SOUL CONVERSION

3 John 1:2
> *Beloved, I pray that you may prosper in every way and [that your body] may keep well, even as [I know] your soul keeps well and prospers.*

That whole chapter of Third John is about the soul, and several other scriptures come to mind about our souls as well (see especially Hebrews 4:11-16 and Psalm 19:7-12).

What is our soul? Our soul is the part of us by which we think and make decisions. But the soul is like a computer. What it is being fed will determine what it does and how it does it.

Our soul can receive either positive or negative input. It can receive either truth or deception. All it knows is what it is being fed, and it will react accordingly.

How is our soul fed? Our souls are fed by what comes into our eye gate, our ear gate and through the imagination of our minds, that which we entertain. The only safety net one has for a healthy and prosperous soul is to keep oneself in God's Word and always welcome the Spirit of Truth, in

Selah Moments

which there is no error. In other words, fill yourself with reading and meditating on the Word of God and maintain the Spirit of Truth in your daily life. That is the only way to guarantee prosperity, success and permanent safety.

Selah!

23

STEP UP, STEP OUT AND STEP OVER!

Joshua 1:9
> *Have I not commanded you, be strong, vigorous and very courageous. Be not afraid nor dismayed, for the Lord your God is with you wherever you go.*

Success in the Promised Land came only after Joshua stepped up to the call, stepped out into the swelling waters of the Jordan, and stepped over the giants then living in the land. Then and only then was his mission complete, that of possessing the promises of God.

But, after you possess, then you must also maintain. Any house, any city or any business, if is not maintained, begins to deteriorate. The elements begin to slowly eat away at it.

It's time to step up to the call of God, for His plans and purposes for your life. Step out into the shifting waters, even if they are swollen and look scary. Step out in faith. The Lord will honor you and still the stormiest waters for your sake.

Selah Moments

Then, step over into victory against the giants in your life, ignoring their threats, and dispossessing and destroying their strongholds. Do not be afraid or dismayed, for the Lord your God is with you. Indeed, He is with you every step of the way!

SELAH!

❧ 24 ☙

THE LORD AWOKE

Psalm 78:65-66
> *Then the Lord awakened as from sleep, as a strong man whose consciousness of power is heightened by wine. And He smote His adversaries in the back [as they fled]; He put them to lasting shame and reproach.*

Today our Father would say:

> I am aroused against your enemies. I am aroused against your foes. I am aroused against the injustices you have suffered. I am aroused as a man of war, plunging into battle for the maintaining of your cause. I am awakened to your defense.
> It is I Who will deal with those who deal falsely against you, for I, your Father, watch over My children.

Selah Moments

Oh, House of Judah, the ones by which I have chosen to exalt my name perpetually, Mount Zion, whom I love, yes, I am awakened to deal with those who have dealt unjustly with you!

SELAH!

❧ 25 ☙

WORSHIP BRIDGES THE GAP!

John 4:24
God is a Spirit (a spiritual Being) and those who worship Him must worship Him in spirit and in truth (reality).

Have you ever felt that there was a gap between you and God? While we know that we do not live by feelings and goose bumps, yet there is a sensing of His presence (or lack of it) that cannot be denied. Your spirit man brings this witness that God is present. Believe it or not, we can actually live 24/7 in this atmosphere of God's holy presence, and it is worship that bridges the gap.

Those who worship God must worship Him in Spirit and in truth. His holy presence is just one breath away. Use that breath to worship Him. Start by saying, "Father, I love You," and watch this one effort begin to change your whole atmosphere.

Once your focus is on God Almighty and not yourself or your circumstances, the atmosphere of Heaven will come

Selah Moments

in like a flood, bringing change, first to yourself and then to your circumstances.

We are without excuse. We have too much at our fingertips to fall prey to murmuring, complaining, defeat and discouragement. Joyce Meyer has said: "Praise and be raised!" So, what are you waiting for? Get your praise on! Get your worship on! Bridge the gap! Bring Father, Son and Holy Spirit into your atmosphere!

SELAH!

26

ONESIPHORUS!

2 Timothy 1:16-18

May the Lord grant [His] mercy to the family of Onesiphorus, for he often showed me kindness and ministered to my needs [comforting and reviving and bracing me like fresh air]! He was not ashamed of my chains and imprisonment [for Christ's sake]. No, rather when he reached Rome, he searched diligently and eagerly for me and found me. May the Lord grant to him that he may find mercy from the Lord on that [great] day! And you know how many things he did for me and what a help he was at Ephesus [you know better than I can tell you].

Onesiphorus ... his name meant "profit bringer." Paul made the statement that many had deserted him while he was in prison in Rome, but that was not true of Onesiphorus. This man went looking for Paul. As a matter of fact, many times he aided Paul in Ephesus. For good reason, therefore, Paul prayed that the Lord would grant mercy to the household of Onesiphorus.

Selah Moments

There are not many faithful and loyal people in our world today, and this is true even in the church. Often, if we are suffering, people flee from us. Some remain, regardless of whether things are going well or not. And God is ever mindful of His loyal and faithful stewards. These people are in it for the long haul, even when things are not convenient, nor fun.

Paul was writing to Timothy, admonishing him by using Onesiphorus as an example of a spiritual truth. To Paul, Onesiphorus lived up to his name: PROFIT BRINGER! He brought much profit to Paul, especially in his times of struggle. When everyone else scattered, this profit bringer was there.

Today we can gain much from Onesiphorus: to be loyal and faithful stewards of God for others in the good and in the bad. This is profitable to those in our sphere of influence. Let us be true to God and His Word and also to His servants, in season and out of season!

SELAH!

෨ 27 ෬

BARS OF BRASS ARE BROKEN!

Psalm 107:15-16

Oh, that men would praise (confess to) the Lord for His goodness and loving-kindness and His wonderful works to the children of men. For He has broken the gates of bronze and cut the bars of iron apart.

Isaiah 45:2

I will go before you and level the mountains [to make the crooked places straight]; I will break in pieces the doors of bronze and cut asunder the bars of iron.

These words have been spoken against those who have committed unjustifiable judgements against you, hindering your progress. These hindrances have been all too real. But, today, from this moment on, those bars of brass are broken, and the free flow of God's Spirit is released to you.

Selah Moments

Now you will see, now you will hear, and now you will move swiftly into that which God has called you to be. A freedom of His holy Spirit now flows, and it is unstoppable!

Selah!

～ 28 ～

A BREAKER'S ANOINTING!

2 Samuel 5:20
> *And David came to Baal-perazim, and he smote them there, and said, The Lord has broken through my enemies before me, like the bursting out of great waters. So he called the name of that place Baal-perazim [Lord of breaking through].*

Baal-perazim was the Lord of breaking through, and God proved Himself at Baal-Perazim to David as the Lord of the Breakthrough. Today that BREAKER'S ANOINTING resides in all believers. Use it.

I call this to come forth from the wells of salvation in you: Breakthroughs over relationships, over ministry, over marriage, over finances, over anxieties, over healing, over brokenness, over whatever you need. "Breakthrough, O Lord, we cry!"

Now begin to cry out: "Holy, holy, holy are You, Lord. In Jesus' name!"

SELAH!

29

DON'T MESS WITH MY KIDS!

Zechariah 2:8
> *For thus said the Lord of hosts, after [His] glory had sent me [His messenger] to the nations who plundered you—for he who touches you touches the apple or pupil of His eye.*

You are one of God's kids, and anyone who messes with you messes with God. He who touches you pokes a finger in God's eye. And when you poke God's eye, He gets aroused.

Some of you have been harassed, evil spoken of and slandered. Men have taken advantage of your love, you kindness, and your goodness, stolen from you and made fun of you, but God has been aroused from His holy habitation for your defense.

God Himself, your heavenly Father has given space for repentance, but now justice is being served on your behalf. Begin to give a shout of thanksgiving and praise, for you are being raised above all that the enemy has

Don't Mess With My Kids!

done against you, and your enemy is being put to shame. This enemy you shall see no more.

For your shame, you will receive double honor, and for your pain, you will receive double the Father God's manifested glory!

Selah!

෨ 30 ෬

EMBRACE YOUR DAY

Psalm 118:24

This is the day which the Lord has brought about; we will rejoice and be glad in it.

He is the Ancient of Days (see Daniel 7:9). Before the earth was, God was. Before the day of Creation, God was there. Each day of our lives exists because God exists. Without God, there would be no day. Therefore, we are to live our lives in each day's sufficiency *from* God and *through* Him.

Matthew 6:31-34

Therefore do not worry and be anxious, saying, What are we going to have to eat? or, What are we going to have to drink? or, What are we going to have to wear? For the Gentiles (heathen) wish for and crave and diligently seek all these things, and your heavenly Father knows well that you need them all. But seek (aim at and strive after) first of all His kingdom and His righteousness (His way of doing and being right), and then all these things taken together will

Embrace Your Day

be given you besides. So do not worry or be anxious about tomorrow, for tomorrow will have worries and anxieties of its own. Sufficient for each day is its own trouble.

As God's children, we are not to worry about what we will eat or drink or wear. The heathen worry about these things because they have no covenant with God, the Great Provider. The world spends way too much time thinking and emoting on these things. How blessed we are to know God!

Worry produces stress, anxiety, fear, depression, oppression, headaches, insomnia and much more. How can we avoid such worry? Because our heavenly Father already knows that we have need of these things.

You should not be like the unsaved, who only have this world's system to rely on. If that worked, there would be no fretting by anyone. We know and trust our Father God, Who owns the cattle on a thousand hills. He has all sufficiency for your day, to provide for both you and yours.

God is the One who makes crooked places straight. He is the One who exalts the valley and brings down the mountains, making a straight path for your feet. He is able and available to perform that which concerns you, with divine provision, direction, connection and protection.

Selah Moments

What do you have to do to make all of this happen? Seek His Kingdom, His authority in your life, His principles, and His righteousness (righteous living of a separated, consecrated life *in* Him and *through* Him). When you do this, all the things that the Gentiles seek and that cause them concern, God said, would be *"added unto you"* (KJV) or *"will be given you."* That includes drink, food, clothing, houses, transportation, healing, deliverance and whatever else you need.

Whatever is concerning you, causing you to fret, if you will just seek God with your whole heart, He will take care of it. While you attend to God, He will attend to you. The Scriptures teach:

1 Peter 5:7
> *Casting the whole of your care [all your anxieties, all your worries, all your concerns, once and for all] on Him, for He cares for you affectionately and cares about you watchfully.*

Seeking God assures you of sufficiency in all thingts.

Psalm 37:34
> *Wait for and expect the Lord and keep and heed His way, and He will exalt you to inherit the land; [in the end] when the wicked are cut off, you shall see it.*

Embrace Your Day

Therefore, we are told, we are not to worry about tomorrow. Tomorrow is another day, and the same God who keeps you today will keep you tomorrow.

That's not to say that you will not have troubles. *"Sufficient for each day is its own trouble."* With each new day, troubles will come. But that's okay. God is there to help you overcome them, whatever they happen to be.

Personally, I have prayed many times:

> Father, if I could change this situation, I would have already done it, but, within myself, I find no power to act. So, in Jesus' name, I release it to You. Align what needs to be aligned in me. I trust You with the process. But this I will do: I will seek Your face and give You praise. You are my Strong Tower, my Defense, my Shield, the Glory and the Lifter of my head, my Sustainer in troubled times and my soon-coming King.
>
> In You is my portion, my inheritance of covenant health, wealth and prosperity, well-being here on earth and eternal life in the hereafter. Whatever is in Heaven is mine in earth. So, despite the evil that lurks in the day, I am hidden in You. And this day is an empowering day of your Holy Spirit presence to lead, guide, instruct, promote and favor my day.

Selah Moments

For this I bow the knee of my heart to a faithful and true God in whom I commit the keeping of my soul, as a faithful Creator. And I, therefore, embrace my day, acknowledging You in all my ways, that You may direct my thoughts.

How about you, friend?

SELAH!

31

FRET OR FAITH?

Mark 4:39

> *And He arose and rebuked the wind and said to the sea, Hush now! Be still (muzzled)! And the wind ceased (sank to rest as if exhausted by its beating) and there was [immediately] a great calm (perfect peacefulness).*

Jesus was in a boat with His disciples when a huge wind storm arose, and the sea suddenly became boisterous, rocking their boat to the point that it felt like it was going to capsize and drown them all. In that moment, Jesus stood up in His authority and rebuked the winds, saying, *"PEACE! BE STILL!"* or *"Hush now! Be still!"*

What happened next? *"The wind ceased ... and there was ... a great calm."* Oh, I like that.

It is the enemy's job to create storms in our lives, to rock our boats and threaten us with death and destruction. He does this to rattle our emotions and bring fear, aggravation and all sorts of soul dilemma. Sometimes it actually seems that we are going to drown, to die, but feelings and emotions are fickle. They can make every situation of life seem boisterous, fearful and frustrating.

What can we do? Jesus is our Prince of Peace, and He is in the boat with us. Just as He did that day, we can use the authority of His name and declare our emotions to be still and remain in peace.

Jesus next asked the disciples:

Mark 4:40
Why are you so timid and fearful? How is it that you have no faith (no firmly relying trust)?

When the next storm comes in your life, know that you are being tested for the Word's sake (see Mark 4:17). It is the Word of faith that calms emotions and gives us the assurance of God's promise of provision, protection and sustenance.

When you find yourself fretting, recognize that the enemy is rocking your boat, trying to cause fear and aggravation. Stand in your authority in faith and declare, "Peace be still!" to your emotions. Then, experience the calmness, the peace that passes all understanding!

SELAH!

∞ 32 ⊗

FINE-TUNE DISCERNMENT

Isaiah 60:2
For, behold, the darkness shall cover the earth, and gross darkness the people: but the Lord shall arise upon thee, and his glory shall be seen upon thee.

We are now living in that season of gross darkness and deception of which the Scriptures speak. The Antichrist spirit is already in the world, and evil spirits are at work, trying to change our Christian culture to a culture of sadistic immoral rights, practicing that which is against nature.

Not only has the enemy been successful at this, but now he wants to infiltrate the hearts and minds of our children. For the sake of social acceptance, our children are becoming lovers of self and not lovers of God.

This new generation is being taught that there are other ways to God except through Jesus. These deceptive strategies are no longer hidden. They are out in the open for all to see. Some, however, are more subtle and less easily discerned.

Selah Moments

There are those who are quoting the Scriptures to prove their point. They are possessed of seducing spirits, having a form of godliness, but they deny the power thereof.

But is this really anything new? This is exactly what Satan did in the Garden of Eden. He twisted God's words and made Eve question what God was really saying. He did the same thing to Jesus in His wilderness experience. He even quoted the Scriptures, insisting, *"It is written!"* But Jesus, Who is the Word in the flesh, knew the whole counsel of God and spoke out the balance of the Word that Satan had used only parts of to tempt Him.

Today is no different. We need to fine-tune our discernment of the subtle use of the Scriptures, making sure that the whole counsel of the Word is present. Otherwise, this subtle demonic spirit that can quote scripture could lead us astray.

How can we fine-tune our discernment?

- Study to show yourself approved.
- Spend time in the secret place with God.
- Become familiar with God's voice and not that of another.
- Pay attention to small promptings, that inner voice of the Holy Spirit.
- Check your check!
- Beware of the many voices and the many teachings.
- Don't accept anything that is scripturally unsound.
- Don't be too quick to join every new movement.

Fine-Tune Discernment

- Don't throw out the baby with the bath water.
- Rightly discern what is being offered.

Hebrews 5:14
> *But solid food is for full-grown men, for those whose senses and mental faculties are trained by practice to discriminate and distinguish between what is morally good and noble and what is evil and contrary either to divine or human law.*

Some things have just enough good in them to make us think they are from God. It is easy to be deceived. Therefore, we must fine-tune our discernment and become a people of wisdom, not quick to fall prey to just anything that comes along!

SELAH!

AUTHOR'S CONTACT PAGE

You may contact Marilyn McDaniels in the following way:

wfscenla@gmail.com

This page must be left blank for the printer's use.

www.ingramcontent.com/pod-product-compliance
Lightning Source LLC
Chambersburg PA
CBHW031414040426
42444CB00005B/561